Survival Basics:

The Most Useful Survival Skills:Food, Shelter, Communication, Curing Herbs

Table of Contents

Introduction: The Will to Survive

The world is one of uncertainty. This wanton instability can be seen on the headline news station's any day of the week. And it really is the Gospel truth that there couldn't be a tie with more war and rumors of war, social discord, and even unpredictable weather. But with all of this doom and gloom what can we do?

Just consign ourselves to our fate and wait for Armageddon to come crashing down on us. Of course not! Because no matter how bleak your circumstances may seem, no matter how much chaos erupts in the world, we can always find the will to survive.

Chapter 1: Finding Water

Regardless of the situation, the first thing that you need to have on hand to survive is a reliable source of water. The human body is an intricate machine, and like any piece of complex machinery it needs certain kinds of fuel in order to run smoothly.

Water is the number one chemical that our bodies need in order to run smoothly. We can only go a few days without this base substance of our body chemistry. Water aids in just about every vital function of the body, being an integral part of blood flow, the digestion of food, and even the regulation of body temperature.

With so much at stake with this chemical compound, no matter what happens, we have to make sure that we have plenty of H2O on hand for it! In many emergency situations local stores will be shut down so that last minute run to Wal-Mart for bottled water may just not be available.

Having that said, you should have your own store bought bottled had already prepped, packed and ready for an emergency. Besides stocking up on store bought water beforehand however—if the spit really hits the fan, and you found yourself without any bottles of water on hand—you can find other ways to locate your water supply.

And believe it or not, your home is full of hidden, already stored water, you probably haven't thought much about. Your home's water heater for example is basically a giant artificial storage tank of drinkable H2O. To access this water all you have to do is place a clean, safe container down under the drain at the bottom of your water heater and then pull the lever on your water heater that releases the liquid. Once pulling this lever water will immediately start draining out of the heater and into your water container.

As your water container fills up you will no doubt notice some pieces of debris floating up to the surface with the consistency of gravel. If you wait a few moments you will find that the material will safely sink to the bottom of the container allowing you to drink the water from the top. You can also take a more proactive approach by pouring your jug through a filter, if you have it, and all of the debris should be removed from the water.

Tapping into your Pipes

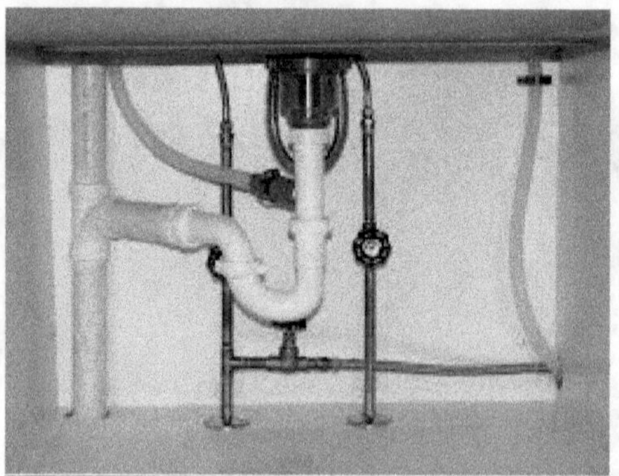

But the water heater isn't the only place that your home is storing water, because to find an inborn water supply all you have to do is look for our pipes! That's right, normal everyday kitchen pipes carry gallons of water ready for consumption at all times. To access the water trapped in your pipes go out and turn off your home's water line so that you can safely remove it.

After you have done this, you can then release the trapped water by just turning your sink's faucet on. Be sure to store as much of this water as you can, because without any ability to get more water from the outside, once your pipes are drained, no more water will be available form your faucets, so make the most of it, storing it in gallon jugs for later use when you really need it.

If you have forewarning, such as before a hurricane or some other major storm, and you know that your water will soon be shutdown, you can take advantage of this warning by filling every sink and bathtub in your home with as much water as you possibly can.

That's right, it might not be appealing to drink out of standing water in your sink (let alone your bathtub) but in an emergency this could be your best means of survival. Just by filling up your bathtub alone you could save yourself many gallons of water. When it comes to storing water in your bathtub however, just keep in mind that there is credence to the initial gross out factor, because the floor of a bathtub even after cleaning it, is usually caked in bacteria.

And if it isn't completely covered with bacteria then it is no doubt coated with potentially harmful chemicals from the cleaning agents you used to sterilize the tub! So having that said any standing water you attempt to drink from your tub should be sterilized either through boiling it or through the use of special cleansing chlorine tablets that will purify the water.

Although your kitchen sink should be a lot cleaner than your bathtub, there is still the potential for a good amount of bacteria there as well too. So be sure to filter, boil or use chlorine tablets when you acquisition the standing water saved in your sinks.

Collecting Water with Rain Barrels

Another great way to requisition yourself some water during a crisis is to make use of the H2O that falls right out of the sky into rain barrels. It's amazing how much water that can be collected simply by putting a barrel outside!

And one of the easiest ways to channel this water would be to stick it right underneath your house's gutters so that all the water that collects on your roof will poll together and pour directly into the barrel below it. Just be sure to sanitize the water by boiling it, using chlorine tablets or even a combination of both.

Emergency Water from your Toilet Tank

Now finally, I've come to the very last place you can look for water in an emergency, I save this one for last because it really is kind of a crap shoot! What am I talking about? Why, storing water in your toilet of course!

One—believe me—most of you are probably ready to retch at just the thought of dipping into your toilet for water. But as harsh as it may seem, if you have went three days without water and feel as if you can barely function you just might be so desperate to do it. So let me explain to you how you can *safely* get water from your crapper!

First of all, when I speak of obtaining drinking water from your toilet, I am in no way referring to the water in your toilet bowel, this water is way to contaminated to even consider. The water that could possibly be used from your toilet actually resides in the tank mounted on the back of your unit. You know—underneath the porcelain lid you lift when your toilet runs too much? That's where possible drinking water could be maintained.

To access this water, shut down your water line, and by all means, do not flush the toilet! Flushing the toilet would immediately deplete this last water resource. So shut off your water, don't flush the toilet, lift the tank's lid and begin gathering it up into empty water bottles.

You can use gloves if you like to achieve this task. After gathering the water, transfer them form the water bottles through a filter, and boil or use chlorine to sterilize the water you have obtained. As desperate as some of these measures may seem, they are all ways that would serve you well, so that you can find water in an emergency.

Chapter 2: Finding a Good Meal

Many of us have probably never experienced real hunger. Sure we may have had our stomach growl a bit if we skipped lunch but we were never painfully hungry from not eating for a week. Short of an eating disorder—most of us in our abundantly blessed modern civilizations have not experienced extreme hunger. But even if a crisis disrupts our content civilized life—it still doesn't mean that we have to go hungry. Knowing how to pack emergency food is the difference between thriving and suffering during a time an emergency.

Canned Food

One of the best ways to store food for indefinite periods of time is to can them. The canning method has been with us for quite some time, and it is still virtually unbeatable when it comes to long term storage.

To get started with this craft of survival, find yourself some classic glass canning jars, many of them have the word "Mason" written on the front just like the included illustration demonstrates.

These jars are initially sealed by the "screw band" that closes over the jar just like a container of peanut butter. One difference between this lid and your peanut butter and jelly lid however, is that it comes in two parts; the screw band and a circular metal top. The top piece you place on top of the jar while you screw the peanut butter type "screw band" over it, closing the lid on the jar. This only the first step however, and at this point your jar is by no means "canned".

To actually seal your jar in proper canning fashion you are going to need to apply intense heat to permanently seal the jar for storage. The most common means of doing this is to use a "pressure canner". This method works by placing your jars in a rack and dipping it into pan of boiling water. For this method to be effective, the water needs to be at least five inches high. Maintain a temperature of at least 180 degrees.

After your cans have been pressurized let them cool down gradually, this is for two reasons; number one so you don't unnecessarily burn yourself and number two so you don't inadvertently cause your jar to crack open or rupture its seal, because an abrupt drop in temperature could do just that. So let the cool own process happen slow and naturally, don't stick it in the fridge, just let the cans sit out at room temperature and slowly cool off.

Root Cellars

Another c method of storing food besides canned goods is to utilize the natural coolness of the Earth through a root cellar. The practice has been around for thousands of years, and it is still effective to this day.

The most common way to create a root cellar in your home is to employ your basement, or rather your basement's corner. All you have to do is board up one corner with some plywood, allow for some ventilation and you have an instant root cellar to store your food in.

Other methods of creating root cellars are even more basic. One of my personal favorites is the "trashcan" root cellar in which you simply bury a metal trash can up to its lip in the ground and then drop in a soft cushioning material like grass, followed by the veggies you are trying to store, followed by anther laycr of grass or leaves.

Just put the metal lid back on this trash receptacle and it's the perfect outdoors root cellar! The main thing with root cellars is to make sure the temperature stays stable. To aid you in keeping track of this it would be a good idea to keep a thermometer near the area you are using for the cellar.

Hunting and Foraging for Food

These are all great methods of preserving food, but what about when your supply runs out, becomes spoiled, or otherwise inaccessible? Then you would have to go out and gather fresh food on your own.

This means you would need to know how to hunt and forage for your own sustenance directly from the environment. In some urban environments this may be easier said than done, but even in the city, there are some wild resources that you can still come by, and when foraging for wild plants, the Dandelion is the first thing that comes to mind.

The Dandelion is known for its bright yellow decorative flowering, but this is know flower, the Dandelion is actually a weed and it is for this reason that you can find this plant popping up just about anywhere. The other good news is that the Dandelion is extremely nutritious. Grab as many of these Dandys as you can, take them home, and boil them as a kind of soup, the taste really isn't all that bad, and the nutritional value is even better.

Mushrooms are another wild food that is also quite ubiquitous and most people can find these little fungus gems right in their backyard. Just be careful with these guys because some of tem could be poisonous; only eat them if you have some sort of reference from which you can ascertain the type of mushroom you have picked. It's always better to be safe than sorry.

Another easy way to get some food right in your own backyard would be to set up a small squirrel trap, even in the big city squirrels can be found all over the place, so it wouldn't hurt to give it a shot. One of the easiest ways have creating these traps is to take a stick and using it to prop up a big rock or cement block and then put some sweet smelling food underneath it. Sooner or later a little critter will come sniffing around the area under the rock.

After nosing around for a bit the little guy will eventually bump into the stick knocking the rock down on his head. May seem a little bit cruel, but when it comes down to survival the squirrel's sacrifice will help to keep you alive. Heck even a New York subway rat might keep you going! (Just kidding, I wouldn't go quite that far!) Any small animal you catch needs to be immediately dressed, meaning that it needs to have its internal organs removed.

To do this make a small vertical cut through the animal's stomach and then simply shake the organs out of its carcass. It may not be pretty, but it is survival. Now just skin the animal's body, remove its head and its ready to be cooked. If nothing else you can just skewer the carcass on a stick and roast it over an open flame. Your reward for your efforts will be the great taste that freshly roasted meat can bring. These are just a few ways you can find a good meal during a disaster!

Chapter 3: Making Your Own Survival Shelter

Making Mud Walled Earth Dwellings

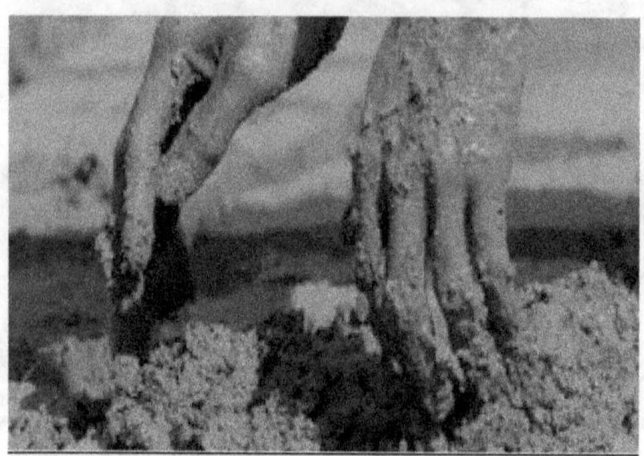

If you find yourself in the crosshairs of crisis with no roof over your head, the best thing you could do is to duck down and start scooping up some dirt. Because as it turns out, "Earth Dwellings" made out of mud and the dirt of the ground are one of the best ways to make a stable and sustainable shelter just about anywhere on the planet. All you need is soil that consists of a 30% gravel/70% sand mixture which is the most common type of dirt found.

To get started just take some water to wet the ground and just like clay pull the material right out of the soil shaping it into brick-like shapes. After fashioning your mud bricks simply put them into the sun and they will bake and become hard. Just make as many of these bricks as you need to start building the walls of your new shelter right on top of the bare ground. Once your walls are as high as you would like, gather up as many long sticks as you can and start placing them across the roof of your structure.

Now take some more mud and smooth it over the sticks and the top of your walls and let it dry in the sun. This will help bond the sticks to the structure. After you have done this you can then gather up leaves and grass and throw them on top of the mud structure adding more wet mud on top. Again let your mud house dry in the sun until it becomes one solid structure.

Making a Ti-Pi

Another great blast from the past when it comes to shelters for humanity is the Ti Pi. These iconic structures at one time were all over the North American plains as the homes of Native Americans. These dwellings are nice because they were made to be mobile. So if you are in a disaster zone and things in your area get worse, with a Ti-Pi you have to benefit of taking your shelter right along with you!

At its core the Ti-Pi is simply three strong branches of about 4 feet in length stood up together in a tripod formation. These branches are then tied together by a piece of cloth or rope. With this frame structure up, simply drape some heavy blankets over the sticks until whole unit has cover. This my friends, is a Ti-Pi! One of the best shelters ever known to man!

Manufactured Tents

Of course just because it's an emergency doesn't mean you have to make your own shelter. There are several kinds of pre-manufactured tents that you can take with you that would be of tremendous benefit. Mimicking the classic Ti-Pi structure, the commercial "ridge tent" consists of two poles at the ends of the tent that hold the structure up. Creating an "A" shaped design this structure is great to keep you dry and out of the rain.

Even better than this though are the "instant tents" that you can literally just pack right in your backpack. (Now that's survival prepping!) The tent is neatly folded along a coiled frame, flattened into one circular package.

Just sett this bad boy on the ground, pull its release mechanism and it will instantly pop right up into a full sized tent! These tents are available online and at most department stores. There is nothing more essential to your survival than a roof over your head, so don't neglect to think about securing your shelter!

Chapter4: Essential Emergency Communication

This is a test. This is a test of the Emergency Broadcast system! Have you ever heard those words over the radio or perhaps flashing across your TV screen? This is the classic phraseology of the Emergency Civil Communication system of the United States.

Normally, during an emergency this would be the first line of communication that people in North America would hear. But what if the civil structure of where you live is suddenly so severely impacted by disaster that it ceases to function. Then my friends, you may have to get a bit more proactive in your own emergency communication! In this chapter we will cover some of your best options in emergency communication.

Ham Radio

The best thing about Ham Radio is their versatility. The work horses of broad band, Ham Operators can get their message out there even with extremely threadbare infrastructure. The fact is, Ham operators serving as multiple relay stations among each other, create their own vital infrastructure as independent broadcasters. Bouncing their signals from multiple locations, even if one part of the country goes completely dark, the other functioning operators can make up for the slack.

In order to work your own Ham Radio you will have to setup what is called your, "Rig" which consists of a transmitter and receiver. After this just get some headphones and a good microphone.

And if you are in a real pinch you could even use your headphones for both. Because once you plug headphones into the mic jack the left ear will instantly turn into a receiving headphone! It can be a nuisance to have to switch back and forth, but in an emergency it could be a lifeline in order to get your message out.

Walkie Talkie Radios

Did you ever stare at the security guard at your local mall chatting happily on his walkie talkie and wished you had one? These communication devices are invaluable during an emergency that funds other more mundane ways to speak limited. The walkie talkie works through a basic, all-in one radio receiver and transmitter built directly into the unit.

You press a button to transmit your message, and as soon as you release the button the walkie talkie then immediately defaults back to a receiver with the voice of whoever you are speaking with emanating directly through the same built in speaker, right back to you. If you are ever worried about some impending crisis you should hook all of your friends and family up with these cheap and easy to use communication systems.

Sat Phones

Even while disaster may loom all across the surface of the Earth, the Satellite Phone has the obvious advantage of being independent from the Earth itself! Able to peacefully float in space far above the fray, even nuclear war would leave Satellite communication unaffected.

The biggest downside of having a Sat Phone is the sheer cost. It costs money to buy the expensive phone and then it costs even more to startup your Sat Phone service. If you do have the cash however, a Sat Phone would give you a definite advantage during an emergency situation and could very well become your most essential means of emergency communication.

Signal Flares

If your need for communication is just to signal others of your presence, emergency flares are one of the easiest and most effective ways to gain the attention of first responders. These flares create an impression light show that can be seen for many miles around. These flares can be accomplished through specially packaged flare sticks, or even a flare gun.

But if you do not have these essential commodities on you, you could always create your own. This is done simply through starting up three fires in a triangle shape big enough to be noticed from up above. This is standard protocol and any emergency personnel would realize that it is a distress signal asking for help. These flares very well could be essential to your survival.

Citizen's Band Radio or as it is more commonly known "CB" Radio, is probably most well know as the chatter box of truckers traveling down the highway. But it is used by more than just semi-truck drivers.

For the past 50 years it has been the mainstay of police, ambulance, and other transportation services all across the planet. Working on short wave radio frequencies, CB radio works similar to a walkie talkie with all participants communicating in quick starts and stops.

Each participant is given a "handle" sort of similar to a screen name in an internet chat room and each participant has to wait his turn to transmit their message. CB radio works on a shared channel which can slow down communication time, but if all other communication systems fail, CB radio may still be a viable; albeit slow means to get your message across. I always keep one of these old school talk boxes around just in case the spit really hits the fan.

Traditional Landline Phone

This is the communication tool that people are likely to scoff at the most. But the fact remains; old school landline phone technology may be the most impervious terrestrial communication you come by.

Even though landline phones have declined quite considerably in popularity, the massive infrastructure that made these simple lines of telephone communication possible, do still exist.

And as long as they are still up and running, they can be used to communicate during an emergency. Cellular phones on the other hand are notoriously unreliable during mass panic situations.

Because while the cell phone towers become overloaded by traffic during an emergency causing major backlogs, so much so, that landlines will end up suddenly becoming the fast lane of communication in which you can skate right through the noise.

Manual Crank Radio's

These radio's have been around for a long time and they are truly essential during power outages since they can be powered by a simple hand powered crank attached to their side. By just cranking this thing up with your hand you can generate enough power to at least hear the latest emergency broadcasts of what is happening in your area.

Some even come fully loaded with ports to plug your phones and tablets into the device, making it more than just a radio but a complete hand driven charging apparatus. All of these essential communication methods are important for your survival.

Chapter 5: The Most Essential Curing Herbs for Survival

Herbs have a long history of healing on this planet about 6000 years in fact. Ancient Egypt, Greece, India, and China all used the natural herbs of the ground to heal all of their ailments for centuries.

In recent times, there has been a revival of sorts, and even the pharmaceutical drenched Western World is rediscovering some of these secrets from the past. Whether it is applying leaves to a wound, using powerful scents for aromatherapy, or massaging soothing plant oils into the body for healing, these herbs are essential, and during a crisis, they very well could be essential to your very survival as well.

Chamomile

This has got to be one of my favorite herbs in the whole world. I love this stuff in my tea and drink it all the time. But Chamomile can do much more than soothe a throat, it can also be worn as a poultice to boost the immune system of the sick.

Pressing crushed Chamomile flowers to the skin can bring immediate relief to inflammation and swelling. Condensed forms of Chamomile pressed to the muscles works as a natural relaxant on muscle tissue as well.

And getting back to that Chamomile tea that I love so much, this herb can cure a lot of things in that format as well. In fact, just breathing in the fragrance of steaming hot Chamomile tea can relax us, even loosening tight blood vessels and lowering our blood's pressure just from the powerful scent. This is definitely an essential herb highly recommended to be kept in anyone's survival cupboard!

Aloe Vera

This healing herb is an absolute classic, and I would be remiss not to mention its amazing propensity to heal cuts, scrapes and burs. As a child growing up in St. Pete, Florida, my grandmother used to grow these plants and whenever one of us kids had a sunburn she would dutifully cut off an

Aloe Vera leaf and rub the substance leaking from that leaf right onto our burn. The reaction was immediate because Aloe Vera plants have natural agents that work to sooth burned tissue.

Just apply the gel from these leaves to the skin and it will greatly work to speed up any burs or scrapes on your skin. If you aren't able to grow your own Aloe Vera plants like my grandmother, you could always purchase it from your local health food store in an already processed liquid gel format. No matter how you obtain these precious substance, it can be a real essential asset during an emergency.

Echinacea

This beautiful flower can be quite easily one of the most essential herbs you could ever come by. This curing herb has been used as tribal medicine in Native communities for thousands of years and for good reason.

Echinacea in its natural form is a highly effective anti-biotic and anti-viral agent capable of greatly protecting and boosting the immune system even in times of great duress. To use Echinacea simply grind the flower of this plant into a fine powder, apply as needed and store in a safe container.

Garlic

Garlic is rather common, it can be found in most pantries in most homes. Despite its commonality however, Garlic has been known to do wonders as an immune booster and even as an antiseptic. In powdered or crushed form, by contacting Garlic to the skin the body's ability to heal wounds can be greatly sped up.

I used to just admire Garlic for the amazing herbal ability it had on top of my spaghetti! But I have since learned that this classic herb is much more essential than just being a pasta seasoning! All of the herbs mentioned in this chapter could be of great use to you no matter what situation you may face!

Conclusion: A Solution to Any Emergency

I may just be channeling my inner MacGyver but I truly believe that with just a little bit of patience and preparation you can be ready for just about anything. We live in a world of mounting challenges and hardships but if we face these struggles with determination and an open mind we can meet them head on. In this book I have highlighted some of some of the most important essentials of survival; shelter, food, water, communication, and herbal medicine.

But the most important tool for survival you could ever have is that 3 pound hunk of meet in your skull. The human brain is the most comprehensive learning tool that Mother Nature has ever bestowed and when used efficiently can easily provide you with a solution to any emergency. I hope that this book has helped you to develop that mindset. Thanks for reading!

FREE Bonus Reminder

If you have not grabbed it yet, please go ahead and download your special bonus report
"Preppers Survival Guide. Proven Tactics For Armed Incounters!"
Simply Click the Button Below

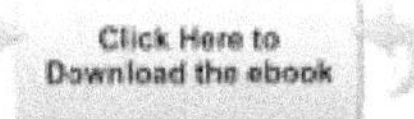

OR Go to This Page
http://preppersliving.com/free

BONUS #2: More Free & Discounted Books & Products
Do you want to receive more Free/Discounted Books or Products?
We have a mailing list where we send out our new Books or Products when they go free or with a discount on Amazon. Click on the link below to sign up for Free & Discount Book & Product Promotions.
=> Sign Up for Free & Discount Book & Product Promotions <=

OR Go to this URL
http://zbit.ly/1WBb1Ek